Vogue Cocktails

HENRY McNULTY

Illustrations by Dolores Fairman
and from the Vogue archive

CONDÉ
NAST
BOOKS

Text copyright © 1982 The Condé Nast Publications Limited.
Illustrations copyright © 1993 Dolores Fairman.

The right of Henry McNulty to be identified as the author of this work
has been asserted by him in accordance with the Copyright Design
and Patents Act, 1988

First published in 1982 by Octopus Books Limited
This edition published in 1993 by Condé Nast Books
Random House, 20 Vauxhall Bridge Road, London SW1V 2SA

5 7 9 10 8 6

Designed by Write Image Ltd

Illustrations by Dolores Fairman
Picture Research by Shona Wood

Set in Perpetua and Avenir
Printed and bound in Singapore by Tien Wah Press (Pte) Ltd.

A catalogue record for this book is available from the British Library

ISBN 0 09 187812 8

Contents

Introduction **4**

Champagne **14**

Gin **22**

Vodka **30**

Whisky **38**

Rum **46**

Brandies and other spirits **52**

Punches **64**

Index **78**

INTRODUCTION

What makes people like to serve and to drink cocktails? There are many other beverages to pick from – enough to satisfy all tastes, you might think.

Mixed drinks have existed since before the time of the Greeks, who invented retsina, mixing wine with resin to preserve it and for its taste's sake. Spiced wines, and those flavoured with other ingredients, were known long before alcoholic spirits came to Europe. The mixing of alcohols with good tastes is a mild form of self-fulfilment: a comparatively easy way to satisfy the creative urge, and a delight when the results are taken judiciously.

The modern versions of these relaxing, sociable concoctions are said to have been first compounded by Americans. During the arid years in the US, when no liquor was legal, a great deal of 'creative thinking' was devoted to inventing new and imaginative formulae to make what alcohol could be found into something drinkable. The skill and originality of those pioneers has been honed by experts to palate-pleasing sharpness.

This little book is intended to encapsulate some of the wisdom of our suffering forebears, allowing you to test both old and new recipes so that, whether fledgling or experienced cocktail maker, you will find it easier to take off, with no fear of flying, from the cocktail nest.

Cocktails are usually made with spirits as a base, plus flavours. Those can come from herbs, spices, fruit juices or other spirits. Most sophisticates prefer their drinks strong – more spirit, less flavouring. Less experienced tipplers like them the other way around. You can cater for either by altering the potency of most recipes to suit the drinker, or yourself.

Some cocktails can be made ahead of time and kept in the refrigerator. The number one favourite cocktail, the Dry Martini, even improves with age, as long as it is kept cold, but separate from ice, until served. Cocktails must be icy cold. Other types of mixed drinks, like grogs, should be hot.

Equipment

If you are to be a relaxed, efficient host, you will find certain basic equipment useful:

1 Good corkscrew
2 Bottle opener
3 A double-end measuring cup
4 A bar shaker with two parts and a strainer
5 A small wooden cutting board for citrus fruit slicing, plus a serrated knife
6 A medium and a large glass mixing jug
7 A long-handled spoon for mixing
8 Bottle sealers for carbonated mixers
9 Fruit juices should be fresh, so a squeezer is handy
10 An insulated ice bucket, big enough to hold at least two trays of ice cubes
11 Ice tongs
12 Champagne tweezers

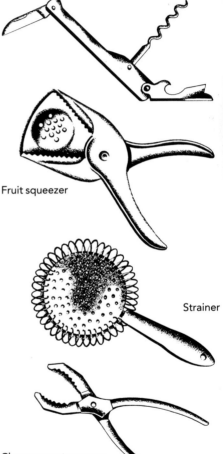

Corkscrew with bottle opener

Fruit squeezer

Strainer

Champagne tweezers

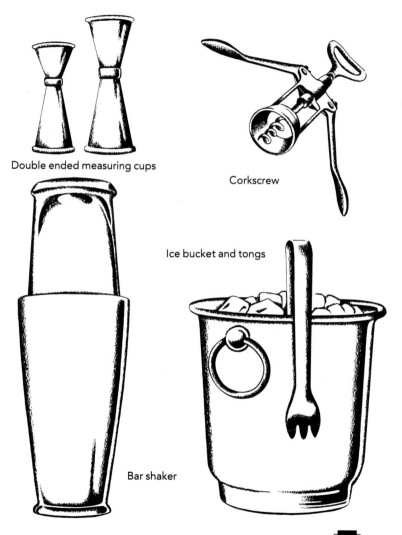

Double ended measuring cups

Corkscrew

Ice bucket and tongs

Bar shaker

Glassware

Use the best glasses you can afford – graceful, thin. I tend to favour stemmed wine glasses for nearly all types of mixed drinks and wine. Even whisky is nice in a stemmed glass. The stem allows you to hold it without heating the contents with your hand. In fact, if you hold the glass by its base, you keep the drink completely isolated from body heat. However, tradition does suggest certain shapes of glass for certain drinks. Glasses should be kept spotless; shining clean. They should never be filled to the brim. Here are the most useful classic shapes:

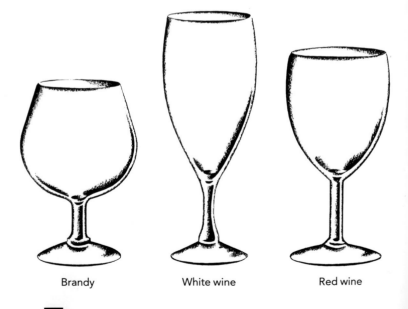

Brandy   White wine   Red wine

Drink	Size	Shape
Brandy	Various	Very round bowl with short stem.
White wine	4 ounce (120ml)	Tulip-shaped bowl, elongated stem.
Red wine	4 ounce (120ml)	Rounded bowl, shorter stemmed.
Highball (tall)	12 ounce (375ml)	Straight or slightly slanted sides; for whisky, collin's, julep.
Old Fashioned	6 – 10 ounce (175 – 300ml)	Squat, flat-bottomed sloping sides.
Liqueur	1 ounce (30ml)	Various shapes, usually small and short stemmed.

Highball   Old fashioned   Liqueur

Drink	Size	Shape
Cocktail	4 ounce (120ml)	V-shaped, straight-sided, stemmed; or a wine glass.
Champagne	4 ounce (120ml)	Tall, slim tulip or flute shape, stemmed. (The old-time flat, stemmed saucer is not very practical – lacks balance and spills contents easily.)
Sherry	2½ ounce (75ml)	Copita – tapering, tulip-curved, short stem. (The wasp-waisted old-time glass is too tiny, and gives no chance to savour aroma.)

Cocktail   Champagne   Sherry

Stocking a bar

You will need a basic supply of goodies with which to fill your glassware if you aspire to fame as a good provider. You really get taste-value for money spent on liquor, so buy the best ingredients: spirits, liquors, wines, flavourings and decorations. Your bar should hold at least:

Whisky
Gin
Vodka
Angostura bitters
Cognac brandy
Crème de Cassis
Crème de menthe
Curaçao
Ginger ale
Grenadine
Vermouth
Soda water
Tonic water
Tomato juice

Simple syrup (made by boiling 2 parts of sugar with one of water for 5 minutes. Bottle and keep in the refrigerator. Simple syrup solves the dissolving problem. A spoonful of syrup equals one of sugar.)

The bar is ready to handle a bigger variety of cocktails if you also have:

Apricot brandy
Benedictine
Chartreuse
Champagne
Cointreau
Crème de cacao
Drambuie
Eau-de-vie
Galliano
Grand Marnier
Kummël
Maraschino
Pernod
Tequila
Triple sec
Swedish punch (rum)

And keep on hand
Lemons
Limes
Eggs
Oranges
Castor sugar

Measurements

Some experts insist on exact measurements. I consider this not always necessary, but it is a good way to begin your cocktail-making career. Later you can experiment with quantities. You should know what measuring terms mean:

Pony	1 ounce (30ml).
Jigger	1$\frac{1}{2}$ – 2 ounces (45 – 60ml). (I consider less than 2 ounces an insult to your guests!)
Wine glass	4 ounces (120ml).
Highball or Collins	8 – 12 ounces (250 –375ml)
Dash (variable)	Usually 3 drops ($\frac{1}{4}$ teaspoon) for a 'light dash'.
Barspoon (or teaspoon)	About $\frac{1}{6}$ ounce (5ml).
Pinch	Less than $\frac{1}{6}$ teaspoon. (Literally what you can pinch between finger and thumb.)

Quantities

You should get about 13 2-ounce (60ml) drinks to a bottle, or six to eight servings from a bottle of champagne or wine. In mixing a large quantity, say of Martinis, for a party, you would need 3 bottles of gin to a quarter bottle of vermouth to produce between 50 and 60 cocktails. Three drinks per person is an average consumption to allow for at a party; or about half a bottle of wine per person, if you serve only wine.

INTRODUCTION

Types of mixed drinks

The occasion often dictates the kind of drink to use – the weather, your mood, the numbers. The following list may help you to decide what to offer your guests:

Cocktail	Usually a basic liquor plus vermouth, bitters and other flavours. Always cold.
Collins	Lemon or lime juice, spirits (usually gin, rum, whisky, brandy), sugar, soda water.
Cooler	Long, iced, summery drink made with a basic liquor or sherry, port, or wine, lemon, sugar and soda water, with ice.
Flip	Whole egg, whisky, or apple brandy, or cognac, or rum in a blender.
Frappé	Pouring drink over cracked ice.
Highball	Spirits served with ice, soda water, ginger ale, or colas.
Julep	Fresh mint and bourbon whiskey.
Punch	Hot or cold, usually with fruit and sugar, combined in spirits or wine.
Sling	Spirits (usually gin, rum, whisky) poured over ice, dissolved sugar, lemon juice, bitters.
Sour	Spirits shaken with lemon or lime juice, sugar (often with the white of an egg).
Toddy	Spice (cinnamon, clove, nutmeg, lemon peel) in a glass with a spirit, with hot water.

Serving

Cocktails are usually served before meals, but have one whenever the impulse hits you. The objective in serving them to friend or foe is relaxation and enjoyment – not to knock them out. To be fair, it is both polite and wise not to pour with too heavy a hand.

Stir or shake? To achieve the proper degree of chill, all drinks made with clear ingredients should be *stirred* with ice – not shaken. Those with fruit juices, on the contrary, should be *shaken* so as to mix the spirit and the fruit properly. The harder the shake, the colder and better they'll be. Cubes of ice are best for an undiluted drink; crushed or shaved ice when sipping a flavourful concoction through a straw, with a straight liquor, or a mint julep. Be sure your ice is fresh and clear.

It may be thought, in view of that well-known incident in the Garden of Eden when Eve turned Adam's head with an apple and they lost Paradise, that apples are the most seductive things to eat or drink. Not so! Champagne, and even its lowlier cousin, sparkling wine, is not only, like diamonds, 'a girl's best friend', but is enormously appealing to the male of the species as well. During a long career of attendance at receptions of various kinds, I have noted confirming phenomena. When faced with a choice between strong drink or the possibility of 'drinking stars' in the form of comparatively light champagne, a majority of people, male or female, will pick champagne.

Perhaps this is because, as the French specialist Dr E.A. Maury implies, champagne is not just a pretty taste, it is also good for you because of its 'euphoric effect on the psyche, without the disadvantages of classic tranquillizers'.

As to sparkling wines, the choice among them is wide, and often very good. There are French 'mousseux', German 'sekt', Spanish 'cava', Italian 'spumante', and American 'champagne', among others, all in competition with the one-and-only, and still world champion, original French champagne.

Champagne is the wine for special occasions, on its own. But it has an important place in the mixed drink world also. One simple idea is to mix equal parts of a good champagne with a fine red burgundy. Add a few strawberries, and top the whole with cream. Adding cream may sound like gilding the lily, but there are people who like cream with, or on, or in, everything, are there not?

When it comes to mixing champagne in a cocktail, apart from a Champagne Cocktail itself, or with orange juice in a Mimosa, I would use sparkling wine. 'Sparkle' is what you really want, and the quality of a delicate wine like champagne tends to get lost among the flavours of a cocktail, so sparkling wines are a sensible substitute. They are also less expensive.

Bellini

- *2 ounces (60ml) peach juice (squeezed from fresh peaches)*
- *4 ounces (120ml) ice-cold champagne*
- *1 dash grenadine if desired*

Mix the ingredients in a large wine glass. Commendatore Cipriani, of the Venetian hotel family, invented the above recipe for one of the first Venice Biennale art fairs. (See Titiani page 21)

Black Velvet

- *½ champagne*
- *½ Guinness*

Half fill a tall glass with cold Guinness. Fill the remainder with chilled champagne (carefully, so it will not fizz up and waste precious drops).

Blue Champagne

- *4 dashes blue curaçao*
- *1 orange slice*
- *4 ounces (120ml) champagne (chilled)*

Swish the curaçao around the sides of a wine or champagne glass. Pour in the champagne and add an orange slice for decoration. This is a speciality from the beautiful Flemish town of Ghent.

Buck's Fizz

- *1 ounce (30ml) fresh, chilled orange juice*
- *1 dash grenadine if desired*
- *3 – 4 ounces (90 – 120ml) Bollinger champagne*

Pour orange juice into a large wine glass, add a dash of grenadine. Fill with chilled champagne. The original of this drink was invented at Buck's Club, London, where they insist that the only champagne to use is Bollinger.

Champagne Cobbler

- *½ teaspoon lemon juice*
- *½ teaspoon curaçao*
- *1 slice lemon*
- *2 – 3 ounces (60 – 90ml) champagne*

Half fill a large wine glass with cracked ice.
Add lemon juice and curaçao. Stir. Add orange slice and fill ⅔ full with champagne.

Champagne Cocktail

There are several versions of this famous drink. The two I favour, and the simplest to make and best, to my mind, are:

Version 1
- 1 lump sugar
- 1 dash Angostura bitters
- Twist of lemon peel
- 2 – 3 ounces (60 – 90ml) champagne

Place a small sugar lump (or ½ teaspoon granulated) in a champagne glass with a small dash of Angostura bitters. Add a twist of lemon peel. Fill glass ¾ full with iced French champagne. (All measures are small to protect the qualities of the wine itself.)

Version 2 (equally easy)
- 1 ounce (30ml) brandy
- 4 ounces (120ml) iced champagne
- 1 twist orange peel

Pour brandy into a champagne glass, fill ¾ full with cold champagne. Twist orange peel over the top to release the oil. (Do not drop peel into glass.)

Champagne pick-me-up

- *1 ounce (30ml) brandy*
- *3 dashes curaçao*
- *3 dashes Fernet Branca*
- *Champagne*
- *Lemon peel*

Place first three ingredients in a white wine glass. Fill the glass with champagne and place the lemon peel on the top.

Champerno

Ernest Hemingway is supposed to have liked one measure Pernod in a wine glass, which he then filled with champagne, instead of soda water, and drank slowly.

Chicago

- *2 ounces (60ml) cognac*
- *1 dash curaçao*
- *1 dash bitters*
- *Champagne*

Stir in the first three ingredients with ice in a glass jug. Strain into a wine glass and fill with iced champagne.

French '75

- $1^1/_2$ ounces (45ml)
  dry gin
- Juice of $^1/_2$ lemon
- 1 teaspoon castor sugar
- champagne

Mix the first three
ingredients in a tall
glass, half filled with
cracked ice. Fill ¾ full
with cold champagne or
sparkling wine.

Kir Royale

- 4 ounces (120ml)
  champagne
- 1 dash crème de cassis

The Dorchester (like
many good hotels)
makes a speciality of
champagne Kir. This
one is very simple
indeed. Just a dash of
crème de cassis in a
champagne 'flute', and
fill with ice-cold
champagne.

Strawberry Champagne Delight

- *2 cups strawberries (frozen if necessary)*
- *1 cup eau-de-vie de fraises*
- *3 bottles of champagne*
- *Whole, fresh strawberries for decoration*

Slice the strawberries in half. Put in a bowl. Over them pour the eau-de-vie de fraises (or if that is not available, any white fruit brandy like kirsch, framboise or Williams). Steep for one hour. Put a block of ice, or several trays of cubes, in a punch bowl. Strain the strawberries out of the brandy. Pour the liquid, plus the champagne, over the ice. Stir very gently. Add whole fresh strawberries to float on top. (Steeped ones tend not to look nice, but they taste wonderful. Eat them later with cream.) For about 20 people. Serve in a white wine glass.

Titiani

A variation of a Bellini (page 16) substituting the juice of grapes, preferably Concord (or *Vitis labrusca*) grapes, for the peach juice. The grapes should be crushed by hand, but wear rubber gloves, for they stain your skin purple!

GIN

Until recently, the most popular ingredient for cocktail making was gin. Today it is being hard pressed by vodka. However, the cocktail most in demand probably still is the Dry Martini, a really arid drink that seems to appeal especially to men (though I know plenty of lady aficionados as well).

Like most beverages in the world of mixed drinks, this old favourite has been evolving ever since its invention. In the early cocktail days of the 'Roaring Twenties', the formula for a Martini was fairly sweet – half gin, a quarter each of Italian white and red vermouth. Later, after President Roosevelt managed to get the US drinking laws changed, the recipe, according to a famous cookery book author, Irma Rumbauer, had become drier – two parts gin to one vermouth, plus two dashes of bitters and a green olive.

Nowadays, the minimum amount of gin is five parts to one or less of dry French vermouth (and the proportion of gin often raised to ten or more to one) with a twist of lemon peel squeezed over the top. If you have made more Dry Martinis than you need that day, by the way, remove any ice and keep what's left in the refrigerator in a corked or capped bottle for later consumption. The Martini's popularity perhaps lies in its lack of sweetness. It is not in the least bit cloying.

Gin is a distilled, pure grain spirit flavoured with juniper berries, herbs and spices, the formula of which is the secret of each individual gin maker. Basically, however, gin is likely to contain coriander, cardamon, angelica, orris root, and dried lemon and orange peel. It can be drunk immediately after it leaves its still, without ageing. Some gin fans claim it does improve with age.

Gin has one big advantage over its nearest rival, vodka. Gin has taste. When I was in University I was friendly with a bartender who was scornful of us sunbathing: 'Thank the Lawd, I don't have to cook myself in the sun like you. It is much more fun just to sit in the shade and sip gin – like drinkin' flowers'.

Alexander

- *1 ounce (30ml) gin*
- *³/4 ounce (25ml) creme de cacao*
- *³/4 ounce (25ml) cream*

Shake hard with ice in a cocktail shaker. Strain into a large cocktail glass. This has been known also to produce sweet reasonableness when made with brandy.

Bronx

- *3 ounces (90ml) dry gin*
- *1 ounce (30ml) dry vermouth*
- *Juice of ¹/4 orange*
- *Twist of orange peel*

Place the gin and vermouth in a cocktail glass. Top with orange juice and add the orange peel.

Bulldog Cooler

- *2 ounces (60ml) gin*
- *Juice of ¹/2 lemon*
- *1 coffeespoon castor sugar (or simple syrup)*
- *Ginger ale*

Fill a highball glass with ice. Add the gin, lemon juice and sugar or syrup. Top up with ginger ale. Stir and serve.

Cardinal

- 2 ounces (60ml) gin
- 2 dashes dry vermouth
- 4 – 5 drops Campari
- Twist of lemon

The Hotel Cipriani on Venice's Guidecca island serves this having stirred all the ingredients except the lemon twist, in a tall-stemmed wine glass. The twist is twisted over the whole. It is a lovely drink to sip as you look across the Grand Canal towards Piazza San Marco, or anywhere else, too.

Gin Buck

- Lime zest
- 2 ounces (60ml) dry gin
- Ice
- Ginger ale

Drop lime zest into the gin in a tall glass. Add ice and ginger ale. Stir and serve.

Dry Martini

- 2 or 3 ounces (60ml or 90ml) London dry gin
- 1 or 2 drops Noilly Prat, Chambèry or Lillet dry vermouth
- Lemon peel or olive

Stir well with 3 – 4 cubes ice. Pour into 4 ounce (120ml) cocktail glasses. Twist a lemon peel over the drink. Some stop at that, and forbid dropping the peel into the drink. Others, of the old school, replace the lemon peel with an olive. Either way, there is a modern tendency to drink this poured over ice ('on the rocks') without lemon or olive. (If you replace the lemon or olive with a pickled onion, you have a Gibson.)

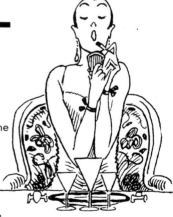

Gloom Raiser

- 1 ounce (30ml) gin
- 1 ounce (30ml) dry vermouth
- 1 dash grenadine
- 1 dash Pernod

Stir gin, vermouth and grenadine with ice. Float Pernod on top in a cocktail glass.

Golden Dawn

- 2 ounces (60ml) dry gin
- 1 ounce (30ml) orange juice
- 1 ounce (30ml) apricot brandy

Shake with ice and serve in a tall glass. A good optimistic cocktail for May Day!

Golden Fizz

- Juice of ½ lemon and ½ lime (1 whole lemon if limes unavailable)
- 1 egg yolk
- 2 ounces (60ml) gin (or the amount your state of mind requires)
- 1 tablespoon castor sugar
- Soda water

Shake first four ingredients well with ice. Strain into a tall glass. Fill two-thirds full with soda water.

Green Lady

- 1½ ounces (45ml) gin
- ½ ounce (15ml) each green and yellow Chartreuse
- Juice of 1 lemon

Shake the ingredients with ice as does Georges Pesce, the barman at Fouquets on Paris's Champs Elysee, and pour into cocktail glasses.

Leave It To Me

- *2 ounces (60ml) gin*
- *1 ounce (30ml) maraschino*
- *1 ounce (30ml) lemon juice (or lemon squash)*
- *1 dash grenadine*
- *1 egg white*

Shake all the ingredients hard for a frothy delight and serve in a large cocktail or wine glass.

Monkey Gland

- *2 ounces (60ml) gin*
- *2 ounces (60ml) Pernod*
- *2 ounces (60ml) orange juice*

Shake all ingredients in a shaker. Serve in cocktail glasses.

Maiden's Blush

- *2 ounces (60ml) gin*
- *1 ounce (30ml) Pernod*
- *Dash grenadine*
- *Twist of lemon*

Stir with ice. Serve in a cocktail glass with twist of lemon.

Negroni

- *1¹/₂ ounces (45ml) sweet vermouth*
- *1¹/₂ ounces (45ml) Campari*
- *1¹/₂ ounces (45ml) gin*
- *Twist of lemon or orange peel*
- *Soda water*

Stir first three ingredients with ice in a tall glass. Serve with lemon or orange peel and topped up with soda water.

Pink Gin

- *1 dash Angostura bitters*
- *2 ounces (60ml) Plymouth gin*
- *2 ounces (60ml) water (or ice)*

Swish the bitters around a 4 – ounce (120ml) glass. Add gin and dilute with water or ice. This is the favourite cocktail of the British Navy. Easy to make, it has a refreshing, 'clean' palate.

Tango

- *1 ounce (30ml) dry gin*
- *1¹/₂ ounces (45ml) dry vermouth*
- *1¹/₂ ounces (45ml) sweet vermouth*
- *2 dashes curaçao*
- *Juice of ¹/₄ orange*

Shake with ice – short and sharp. Strain and serve in an Old Fashioned glass.

Tom Collins

- *Juice of ¹/₂ lemon*
- *Castor sugar to taste (¹/₂ teaspoonful)*
- *2 ounces (60ml) gin*
- *3 – 4 ice cubes*
- *Soda water*
- *Lemon slice*

In a tall glass stir the lemon juice with the sugar. Add the gin and ice then stir again. Fill with soda water or still water. Garnish with lemon slice.

Collins's are nice old-fashioned drinks, relatively easy to make, being nothing more than home-made lemonade, truth to tell, with gin (or vodka or whisky or rum) in them. They are utterly suitable for a hot afternoon's tennis party or after golf.

Wallis Blue

- *1¹/₂ ounces (45ml) gin*
- *1 ounce (30ml) blue curaçao*
- *Juice of 1 lime*

Shake all the ingredients together with ice. Pour into cocktail glasses whose rims have been rubbed with lime pulp. And if you like a sweet touch, dip the rims in castor sugar.

White Lady

- *1¹/₂ ounces (45ml) gin*
- *¹/₂ ounce (45ml) Cointreau*
- *1 ounce (30ml) lemon juice*
- *1 egg white*

The egg white is the Dorchester's way of jazzing up this old favourite. Pour all the ingredients into a shaker and really give it a thorough shaking up. The egg white 'plumps' up the drink (and is a good trick with almost all cocktails – try it with a Bloody Mary) but does not change the taste, nor does it add a calorie! Serve in a cocktail glass.

Russians and Poles, they tell me, drink their vodka (which means 'little water') with much lighthearted speed because they are afraid of becoming drunk on its fumes. It seems you inhale more alcohol than you drink, they claim, by sipping it slowly.

Those inventors and enthusiastic consumers of the fastest selling spirit these days, like it with a 'tear' – that is with the outside of the glass frosty with cold. They also like it to be flavoured and coloured, rather than tasteless and odourless as we seem to in the West.

Vodka in its native lands – Poland and Russia – is served icy cold and straight with caviar, smoked salmon or salt herring. You are supposed to toss your tiny glassful to the back of your throat, gulp it down fast, and take another one immediately. Their excuse is that vodka was supposedly medicinal in medieval times, so they got used to taking small quantities all day long.

The East gets flavour into vodka at home, simply by steeping various herbs in what they buy. You can do the same. Tarragon, honey, chilli peppers, coffee, lemon or orange peel – almost anything that appeals to you – can flavour your vodka. (My preference is for Zubrovka, made with a slip of the zubrovka plant, 'favourite herb of the European bison', in it, giving a subtle, nutty taste, and the palest of green tints.) The procedure is easy. Just put some fresh tarragon or whatever into the bottle and let it sit for a week or two. Red pepper, by the same process, turns it satisfyingly pink.

One Leningrad factory produces vodka in 32 different tastes. In the West it is above all an excellent party mixer because it is flavourless and odourless.

Furthermore, in any cocktail made with gin you may substitute vodka – so the variety of flavours and mixes available to you is practically unlimited. Vodka does not clash with wine. You can start with vodka, switch to wine during the meal, go back to vodka later, and still hold your head hangoverless and high the next morning!

Aqua Marina

- *1 ounce (30ml) lemon juice*
- *1 ounce (30ml) crème de menthe*
- *2 ounces (60ml) vodka Champagne*

Shake all but champagne, with ice. Strain into a tall glass. Top with champagne. A Duke's Hotel invention.

Bloody Mary

- *2 ounces (60ml) vodka*
- *4 ounces (120ml) tomato juice*
- *Juice of ¹/₂ lemon*
- *1 – 2 dashes Worcestershire sauce*
- *1 dash Tabasco*
- *Salt, pepper, celery salt*

Stir hard or shake well with ice. Strain into a glass, or serve on the rocks. You can use canned tomato juice for this. (Schweppes makes a 'tomato cocktail', with the Worcestershire, salt and pepper already in it, if you are that lazy.)

Bullshot

Substitute beef bouillon (canned consommé will do) for the tomato in the above recipe, and you have a Bullshot.

Cooch Behar

- *Ice*
- *2 ounces (60ml) pepper vodka (see page 31)*
- *4 ounces (120ml) tomato juice*

Place two or three ice cubes in an Old Fashioned glass. Add the vodka and tomato juice. Stir gently and serve. (Invented by the Maharaja of that name and place.)

Coloured vodka

You can serve various coloured vodkas by adding herbs, seeds or nuts to your bottle. Saffron turns it yellow; sunflower seeds, mauve; cornflowers, blue; walnut shells, brown.

The Godmother

- *1 1/2 ounces (45ml) vodka*
- *3/4 ounce (25ml) Amaretto (almond liqueur)*

Serve in an Old Fashioned glass, stirred with ice.

Flying Red Horse

- *6 ounces (175ml) orange juice*
- *1 ounce (30ml) vodka*
- *2 dashes Grand Marnier*
- *1 dash grenadine*

Stir with ice and serve in a tumbler.

Green Treetop

- 2 ounces (60ml) vodka
- 2 ounces (60ml) lemon juice
- Sugar to taste
- Dash of creme de menthe
- Mint leaves, chopped

Pour the vodka, lemon juice and sugar over ice. Serve with mint and a drop of creme de menthe in a tall glass.

Hair Raiser

- 1 ounce (30ml) vodka
- 1 ounce (30ml) Dubonnet
- 1 ounce (30ml) Schweppes tonic

Pour the ingredients over the 'rocks', stir and serve in a tall glass.

Harvey Wallbanger

- 2 ounces (60ml) vodka
- 4 ounces (120ml) orange juice
- 1 tablespoon Galliano

Fill a tall glass ¾ full of ice. Add the orange juice and vodka, then stir. Gently float the Galliano on top.

Le Mans

- 2 ounces (60ml) Cointreau
- 1 ounce (30ml) vodka
- Soda water
- 1 slice lemon

Mix the Cointreau and vodka in a tall glass. Add soda water and lemon (as sipped at the 24 hour race).

Lovers' Nocturne

- 1 1/2 ounces(45ml) vodka
- 1/2 ounce (15ml) Drambuie
- 1 dash Angostura bitters

Shake all ingredients well with crushed ice, then strain into cocktail glasses. Best served on a moonlit night with Chopin as background music.

Lucky Jim

- 2 ounces (60ml) vodka
- 1 dash dry vermouth
- 2 dashes strained cucumber juice

Mix with ice. Serve in an Old Fashioned glass.

Mint Collins

- 4 mint leaves
- 2 ounces (60ml) vodka
- Juice of 1 lemon
- Sugar to taste
- Soda water
- Mint sprig to decorate

Crush 4 mint leaves in the mixture of vodka, lemon and sugar in a tall glass. Add ice and soda. Decorate with mint.

Morton's Special

- 2 ounces (60ml) vodka
- 2 ounces (60ml) tequila
- 2 ounces (60ml) orange juice
- 1 dash grenadine

Blend all the ingredients together. Serve in a large stemmed goblet.

Oriental Cooler

- 2 ounces (60ml) gin or vodka
- Juice of ½ lime
- 3 dashes Angostura bitters
- Tonic water

Mix the gin or vodka, lime juice and Angostura in a tall glass. Top up with tonic water.

Raspberry Vodka

- 1 pound (500g) raspberries
- 1 quart (1.2 litres) vodka

Steep raspberries in the vodka for 1 week. Strain and decant. Serve in wine glasses.

Ratafia of Pinks

Collect ½ pound (250g) petals of pinks, and steep for a month in a quart (1.2litres) of vodka with 1 clove and ½ teaspoon cinnamon. Filter the mixture and add a syrup made from 2 cups each of sugar and water. Filter again, and bottle. Serve with ice and soda water, or from a decanter, in wine glasses.

Silver Vodka Fizz

- 2 ounces (60ml) Smirnoff vodka
- Juice of ½ lemon
- ½ teaspoon sugar
- 1 egg white
- Soda water

Shake vigorously with cracked ice. Serve in a tall glass and top with soda water.

Summer of '75

- 2 ounces (60ml) vodka
- 1 ounce (30ml) calvados
- 1 ounce (30ml) apple juice
- 1 dash Angostura bitters
- Orange slice
- Mint sprig

Mix the first four ingredients in a tall glass with ice. Stir. Serve with a slice of orange and sprig of mint as made in Nicol's bar at the Cafe Royal.

Vodkatini Dry

(see Dry Martini recipe, page 25)
- 1 dash dry sherry (in place of vermouth)
- 2 ounces (60ml) vodka (in place of gin)

Vodpacho

- 1 serving of Gazpacho
- 2 ounces (60ml) vodka

For each person simply add the vodka to a soup bowl of chilled gazpacho. An interesting start to a meal.

Watermelon Cooler

- 1/2 water melon
- 3 tablespoons grenadine
- 5 – 6 mint leaves
- 2 ounces (60ml) vodka (optional)

Remove seeds from watermelon. Pulp the flesh in a blender until smooth, then pass through a sieve if you like. Add the grenadine, and fresh mint leaves. Set mixture in a refrigerator for 1 hour or so. Stir before drinking. (The children can have this as it is.) You may like it even better with icy vodka added to each serving.

(Remember: in most recipes for a cocktail made with gin, you can replace the gin with vodka.)

WHISKY

Traditionally whisky – Scotch, that is – was supposed to be dark, peaty and pungent. Since the days when drinkers discovered 'light' whisky, partly influenced by the American market, it has tended to be paler, though not less potent, with a firm, clean palate, and dry, with a less lingering flavour than that of the original blends.

The Americans and Canadians have built up their own varieties of flavours, too, with Bourbons and Rye whiskeys. The Japanese and other nations have also moved in on the act. Blended whisky is today one of the world's preferred beverages.

Most whiskies can double excellently as bases for further blending – in cocktails. However, purists insist that the best way to drink the aged versions, whether of blended Scotch, Malt, Irish, Bourbon or Rye, remains as a straight 'sipping whisky'.

Malt whisky, still very popular with connoisseurs, is the father of the blends we drink today and was born well before the 15th century when the first Scottish records of the beverage mention it. Distilleries then were small, usually sidelines to farming. About 100 years ago an Edinburgh genius named Andrew Usher is credited with being the first to blend malt with grain whisky to reduce its pungency. After that, the demand for the drink grew to international proportions.

Malt whisky is distilled twice from barley in pot stills, over peat fires, using pure spring or 'burn' water. Grain whisky, with which it is blended, is made by a continuous distilling process that produces a lighter-flavoured type of spirit. Both are matured in oak casks for several years to mellow into what we drink today.

Blending is controlled by a 'nose', an expert who smells the aroma, but never actually sips, because the alcoholic content of the spirit overpowers taste buds after a sip or two. Each of the 150 or so distilleries in Scotland has its own secret blending formula – and by law the minimum age of Scotch is three years before it can be sold.

Boilermaker

- *2 ounces (60ml) of whisky, with a beer chaser on the side*

Not quite a mixed drink, but an easy ancient prescription!

Football Fan

- *1 ounce (30ml) Scotch*
- *1/2 ounce (15ml) Cointreau*
- *1/2 ounce (15ml) fresh, unsweetened grapefruit juice*

Shake well with ice then strain into a cocktail glass.

Flying Scot

- *2 ounces (60ml) Scotch*
- *1 ounce (30ml) sweet vermouth*
- *1 teaspoon simple syrup*
- *1 coffeespoon Angostura bitters*

Shake with ice then strain into an Old Fashioned glass.

Fourth of July

- *2 ounces (60ml) orange juice*
- *1/2 ounce (15ml) lemon juice*
- *1 ounce (30ml) Bourbon*
- *1/2 ounce (15ml) apricot brandy*

Shake with ice and serve in an Old Fashioned glass. Good mix for an American bar!

Harry Lauder

- *1 ounce (30ml) Scotch*
- *1 ounce (30ml) sweet vermouth*
- *1 dash sugar syrup*

Stir with ice then strain into a cocktail glass.

Kojak

- 3 ounces (90ml) Bourbon
- 2 ounces (60ml) passionfruit juice
- 1 ounce (30ml) pineapple juice
- 1 dash dark rum

Stirred with a lollipop at the London Hilton.

Ladies

- 2 ounces (60ml) whisky
- 2 dashes Pernod
- 2 dashes anisette
- 1 dash bitters

Stir well with ice, add a piece of pineapple if desired and serve in a cocktail glass.

Loch Lomond

- 2 ounces (60ml) Scotch
- 2 dashes bitters
- Sugar to taste (1 teaspoon maximum)

Shake with ice. Strain into a cocktail glass.

Manhattan (modern)

- 2 ounces (60ml) any type whisky (but preferably American)
- 1/2 ounce (15ml) dry vermouth
- 1 dash bitters
- lemon twist

Stir hard then strain into an Old Fashioned glass. Add lemon twist if you want it.

Manhattan (original)

- ½ rye whiskey
- ½ Italian vermouth
- Dash bitters
- Maraschino cherry
- Slice of orange or lemon

Stir with ice. Serve in an Old Fashioned glass with a maraschino cherry and a slice of orange or lemon.

Mint Julep

Per serving:
- 2 springs fresh mint
- ½ teaspoon castor sugar
- Mint sprigs, to decorate
- 2 ounces (60ml) Bourbon whiskey
- Soda water

Version 1
North America's contribution to world drinking pleasure has a large number of competing recipes. My favourite is: Fill tall glasses with crushed ice. Set them aside until other ingredients are ready. Pluck leaves from fresh mint, crush in a small glass with castor sugar. Add a little soda water, crush again and add the Bourbon whiskey. (Scotch may be used but it alters the taste and is not strictly 'kosher'.) Stir. Strain into ice-filled glasses. Stir with a long spoon until outside of glass is frosted. Decorate with sprigs of mint. Serve.

Version 2
Another method requires you to crush the sprigs of mint in the glass with a spoon; rub mint around inside of glass and discard. Fill glass with crushed ice. Slowly pour in Bourbon. Add dissolved lump of sugar. Do not stir!

Old Fashioned

Original version

- 1 lump sugar
- 1 dash Angostura bitters
- Twist of lemon peel
- 2 – 3 ounces (60 – 90ml) Rye whiskey
- 1 maraschino cherry
- Slice of orange

Place sugar in an Old Fashioned glass with a drop of water to dissolve it. Add Angostura. Spread the softened sugar and Angostura around sides of glass. Add ice cubes and a twist of lemon peel. Fill with whiskey (any type will do, but preferably rye). Stir. Decorate with cherry and orange slice.

Ohio Old Fashioned

- 4 drops Angostura bitters
- 2 ice cubes
- 2 – 3 ounces (60 – 90ml) Bourbon whiskey

Stir in an Old Fashioned glass, fill with water ($\frac{1}{2}$ whiskey, $\frac{1}{2}$ water approximately). No sugar, no fruit. (Some people call the original version 'pickled fruit salad', though I find it delectable.)

Ritz Old Fashioned

- 3 ounces (90ml) Bourbon
- 1 ounce (30ml) Grand Marnier
- Dash lemon juice
- Dash maraschino

Shake all in ice filled shaker. Serve in a chilled glass. (Personally I don't like my glass rims sugar-coated, but if you like them that way, the genuine recipe is served after dipping the chilled rim in sugar and garnishing with a cherry and slices of lemon and orange.)

New Yorker

- *2 ounces (60ml) Bourbon*
- *¹/₂ ounce (15ml) lime juice*
- *¹/₂ ounce (15ml) grenadine*
- *Twist of orange peel*

Shake the first three ingredients with ice and serve in a cocktail glass with a twist of orange peel.

Pink Elephant

- *2 ounces (60ml) Bourbon*
- *1 ounce (30ml) lemon juice*
- *2 dashes grenadine*
- *1 egg white*

Shake with ice and serve in a cocktail glass. (From the London Hilton.)

Rob Roy (Dry)

- *2 ounces (60ml) Scotch*
- *1¹/₂ ounces (45ml) dry vermouth*
- *1 dash Angostura bitters*
- *Twist of lemon peel*

Stir the first three ingredients with ice. Serve with twist of lemon peel in a cocktail glass.

Wild Irish Rose

- *2 ounces (60ml) Irish whiskey*
- *1/2 ounce (15ml) grenadine*
- *Juice of 1/2 lemon or lime*
- *Soda water*

Place the first three ingredients in a tall glass with ice. Fill with soda water.

Scotch Mist

- *Ice*
- *2 ounces (60ml) whisky*
- *Lemon peel*

Fill an Old Fashioned glass with shaved ice. Add whisky (again any type, but preferably Scotch). Drop in peel.

Whisky Sour

- *2 ounces (60ml) whisky*
- *Juice of 1/2 lemon*
- *Sugar to taste*

Mix the ingredients in an Old Fashioned glass.

RUM

'**In rum lies truth**' is an ancient saying from the French Antilles, a small component of the Caribbean's thousands of islands. If that saying is so, those islands must be among the most truthful locations on Earth, for each produces its own version of rum.

Whether influenced in their culture by the French, the Spanish, the British or the Americans, each island or group of islands claims to make 'the best' rum; to enjoy the most sensuous of lifestyles; to bask in breeze-cooled, near-tropical heat; to boast happy, languorous people with hot blood and a congenital allergy to unnecessary effort.

Although rum is manufactured in nearly every country of the world, from the USA to Russia, and from South Africa to Australia, the best does come from the Caribbean. Top of them all, to my mind, is the dry, golden rum from Martinique with St. James as the very best of them. There will be arguments about this, however; from Cuban and Puerto Rican light, dry rums to Jamaican dark sweet ones. Who am I to protest? The truth, as the old adage above says, is that they all make marvellous mixed drinks.

Jamaican rum was the original standard in Anglo-Saxon countries and is still one of the favourites in Britain. In the United States of America, Bacardi, once the pride of Cuba, now made in Puerto Rico and other places, supplies three-quarters of the rum Americans drink.

Not only does rum blend beautifully with other liquors, it goes well with fruit (especially lime) juices. In the islands ('la bas, dan les isles'), it is also used as a medicament for healing wounds, for assuaging headaches and toothaches, to reduce bruises, and to induce euphoria. Rum is made from molasses, for the most part, but a good deal is distilled directly from sugar-cane juice, especially in the French-influenced islands, including Haiti. Matured, aged, straight rum is delicious as a liqueur, or in coffee. Darker rums make good punches, light ones excellent cocktails.

Bacardi Cocktail

- *Juice of 1 lime*
- *1/2 teaspoon sugar*
- *1 1/2 ounces (45ml) light rum*

Stir the ingredients in a shaker before adding cracked ice. Shake hard, then strain and serve in cocktail glasses. (Some recipes call for a dash of grenadine instead of sugar but the original 'true' version of this old favourite scorns 'the pink kind'.)

Bossa Nova

- *1 ounce (30ml) dark rum*
- *1 ounce (30ml) Galliano*
- *1/2 ounce (15ml) apricot brandy*
- *3 ounces (90ml) pineapple juice*

Mix with ice in a tall glass. As served on the Carras Line cruise ship, *Daphne*, in the Med.

Calypso

- *1 1/2 ounces (45ml) Trinidad (or other) light rum*
- *1/2 ounce (15ml) simple syrup (or to taste)*
- *1/2 ounce (15ml) orange juice*
- *1 teaspoon lime juice*

Blend all in a mixer with crushed ice or shake well. Serve in champagne glasses.

Chocolate Cocktail

- 1 ounce (30ml) white rum
- 1 ounce (30ml) dark rum
- 1 ounce (30ml) crème de menthe
- 1 egg white
- 1 ounce (30ml) single cream
- 1 tablespoon dark rum to float
- 1 teaspoon cocoa powder

Shake the first five ingredients with ice. Strain into a tall glass. Float the tablespoon of dark rum on top and sprinkle with the cocoa powder.

Daiquiri (frozen)

- 6 ounces (175ml) medium rum
- 1 tablespoon simple syrup, or 1 teaspoon castor sugar
- Juice of 1 lemon

This classic is whirled in a blender with crushed ice to almost sorbet consistency. Alternatively, omit the ice from the blender and pour mixture over crushed ice in an Old Fashioned glass.

Cuba Libre

- 2 ounces (60ml) dark rum
- Juice of ½ lime, or 1 lemon
- Ice
- Cola drink

Place the first three ingredients in a tall glass and fill with a cola drink.

Euphoria

- 2 ounces (60ml) white rum
- 1 ounce (30ml) grapefruit juice
- ½ ounce (15ml) pineapple juice
- ½ ounce (15ml) curaçao

A tropical tasting drink to be stirred well with ice and served in a cocktail glass.

The Hurricane

- *1¹/₂ ounces (45ml) dark rum*
- *1¹/₂ ounces (45ml) lemon juice*
- *2 ounces (60ml) passion fruit juice*
- *1 teaspoon sugar*

Shake all the ingredients with ice, as they do in the Hotel Portman's Bar Normand. Serve in a tall glass.

Mojito

- *2 ounces (60ml) white rum*
- *5 fresh mint leaves*
- *¹/₂ teaspoon sugar*
- *2 dashes Angostura bitters*

Shake with ice and strain into a cocktail glass.

Piña Colada

- *2 ounces (60ml) white rum or tequila*
- *2¹/₂ ounces (75ml) coconut cream (Coco Ribe or Malibu are brands you can buy ready-mixed with rum)*
- *3 ounces (90ml) pineapple juice*
- *Maraschino cherry*
- *Pineapple*

Whirl the first three ingredients with ice in a blender, or shake vigorously. Pour into a tall glass and garnish with a maraschino cherry and a stick of pineapple.

Paradise

- *3 ounces (90ml) white rum*
- *2 ounces (60ml) apricot brandy*

Shake with ice, and sip from a cocktail glass.

Pineapple Collins

- 2 tablespoons pineapple juice (instead of usual lemon juice)
- 1/2 teaspoon castor sugar
- 2 ounces (60ml) rum
- Soda water
- 1 egg white (optional)

Pour the first three ingredients and egg white, if used, into tall glass with ice and fill with soda water. The white of an egg adds froth.

Planter's Punch

- 2 ounces (60ml) fresh lime juice
- 1 tablespoon simple syrup
- 4 ounces (120ml) dark rum
- Soda water

Place the first three ingredients in a highball glass 2/3 filled with ice. Fill with soda water or plain water.

Ron Cacique

- 1 ounce (30ml) light rum
- 1 1/2 ounces (45ml) Dubonnet
- 1/2 ounce (15ml) lime juice (or lemon)
- 1 dash Angostura bitters

Stir with crushed ice. Strain into cocktail glasses.

Shanghai Cocktail

- 1 1/2 ounces (45ml) dark rum
- 1/2 ounce (15ml) anisette
- 3/4 ounce (25ml) lemon juice
- 2 dashes grenadine

Stir the ingredients vigorously with 3 or 4 ice cubes. Strain into a cocktail glass. A cooling concoction invented in the hot old days just off the Bund.

51

BRANDIES AND OTHER SPIRITS

Brandy, possibly the oldest form of drinking spirit, is made from grape wine. The best brandies are French – cognac and armagnac. After them come quantities of German, Italian and Spanish brandies, Portuguese, some Greek, and American ones.

Wine brandy is a staple in many homes, not only as a fine spirit drink, but as an insurance against illness. Hospitals use brandy as a stimulant. Russian ladies use it for shampoo. The Chinese believe it is good for their love lives, the french for 'preservation'.

Fruit brandies are made by distilling fermented fruit juice, or by macerating the fruit in a spirit. They can be made from fruit with stones, berries, or citrus fruit. Maraschino comes from cherries of the same name. Kirsch is made from distilled cherry juice. Calvados, or applejack, is made from ripe apples crushed and allowed to ferment. The resulting liquid is distilled and aged in wood to give it a golden brown hue. Poire Williams, though white, is a similar product of Williams pears.

Liqueurs are infusions or distillations of herbs, fruit or spices with alcohol. They are delicious for after-dinner drinking on their own, or frappéd, and are usually sweet. They are also excellent as flavouring ingredients in cocktails. Southern Comfort is American whiskey with fresh peach and orange flavouring.

Aperitifs, imbibed on their own before meals or used in cocktails, are a variety of drinks including sherry, vermouth, Campari, Lillet. On the other hand, Fernet Branca is classed as a *digestiv* – to be drunk after a meal or indeed as late as the morning after some over-indulgence. Italians, however, faithfully drink it as an aperitif. Aquavit (herb-flavoured spirit made from potatoes or grain), Pernod (only one of the many spirits flavoured with aniseed) and arrack (made from almost anything including rice or grape juice) should be mentioned in any list of worthy spirits; but perhaps tequila is one of the most remarkable. A few years ago only Mexicans drank it regularly. Now many of the most internationally known cocktails are based on it.

Acapulco

- 1 ounce (30ml) tequila
- 1 ounce (30ml) Kahlua (coffee liqueur) or Tia Maria
- 1 ounce (30ml) dark rum
- 3 ounces (90ml) coconut cream

Shake with ice. Serve in a large glass. A fairly 'block busting' combination! Take care.

Algonquin

- 1 teaspoon baked apple or apple sauce
- 1 lump sugar
- 2 ounces (60ml) applejack (apple brandy)
- Grated nutmeg

Mix first three ingredients in a tall glass. Fill with hot water. Sprinkle with nutmeg.

Clement Cowles

Blue Med

- *1 teaspoon blue curaçao*
- *1 teaspoon Pernod*
- *2 ounces (60ml) vodka*
- *Sprig of mint*

Mix all ingredients with ice then relax with this cool concoction served in a large cocktail glass with a sprig of mint. (Try, also, with a dash of ouzo or Pernod in a glass of orange juice.)

Brandy Sling

- *1 teaspoon sugar*
- *1 dash Angostura bitters*
- *Juice of $^1/_2$ lemon*
- *3 cubes of ice*
- *3 ounces (90ml) cognac*
- *Water*

Put first four ingredients in a tall glass. Fill with plain water. Stir and serve.

B & B

- *1 ounce (30ml) cognac*
- *1 ounce (30ml) Benedictine*

This is simply half brandy, half Benedictine, but the dryness of the drink can be varied according to the amount of brandy you use – the more the drier. Mix and serve either in a brandy glass straight or over crushed ice. (You can buy this, ready-made by the Benedictine people.)

Brandy Smash

- *4 sprigs fresh mint*
- *1 teaspoon castor (or powdered) sugar*
- *Soda water*
- *$1^1/_2$ ounces (45ml) brandy*
- *Mint sprig*

Crush the mint lightly with sugar in an Old Fashioned glass. Add splash of soda water, 2 cubes of ice, and the brandy. Garnish with mint sprig. Stir gently and serve.

Braniff Special

- *1 apple*
- *1 orange*
- *1 peach*
- *Juice of 1 lemon*
- *2 ounces (60ml) kirsch*
- *1 strawberry*
- *Mint*

Slice fruit into a bowl with lemon juice. Pour kirsch over them. Allow to marinate for 10 to 15 minutes. Serve in champagne glasses, decorate with fresh strawberry and 1 mint leaf. (More a meal than a drink! You can also serve with ice cream and Grand Marnier instead of kirsch.)

Café Kirsch

- *1 ounce (30ml) kirsch*
- *1 teaspoon castor sugar*
- *1 ounce (30ml) cold black coffee*
- *White of 1 egg*

Shake with crushed ice. Strain into a large cocktail glass.

Coffee Royale

- *Sugar*
- *Black coffee*
- *2 ounces (60ml) cognac*

Place a lump of sugar in a spoon and set it across a hot cup of black coffee. Soak the sugar with cognac. Let the spoon heat up, then light the cognac and slide it into the coffee. (Or simply pour 1 ounce (30ml) of cognac into a cup of coffee, without the benefit of flaming.) Cream to float.

Crème de Menthe Frappé

- Crushed ice
- 2 ounces (60ml) crème de menthe

Heap a cocktail or wine glass full of ice. Pour the crème de menthe over it until the glass is full. Serve with short straws or sip from the glass.

Crimean Cocktail

- 3 ounces (90ml) dry white wine
- 1 ounce (30ml) Cointreau
- 1 teaspoon grated lemon zest
- Soda water
- Cherries

Place the first three ingredients in a cocktail glass and top with soda. Decorate with cherries.

The Duke

- 2 ounces (60ml) Drambuie
- 2 ounces (60ml) orange juice
- 1 egg white
- Orange and lemon slices

Shake the ingredients and pour into a cocktail glass. Decorate with orange and lemon slices. (From Dukes Hotel, London.)

Greek Manhattan

- 3 ounces (90ml) Metaxas brandy
- 1 ounce (30ml) dark red Mavrodaphne wine

Serve in a cocktail glass with ice.

Golden Dream

- 1 ounce (30ml) fresh cream
- 1 ounce (30ml) orange juice
- 1 ounce (30ml) Cointreau
- 1 ounce (30ml) Galliano
- Orange slice
- Cherry

Shake the first four ingredients with ice. Serve in a tall glass and add a slice of orange and a cherry for decoration. (This is a new invention from the Dorchester's 'The Bar'.)

Hot-T

- 2 ounces (60ml) Cointreau or curaçao
- 8 ounces (250ml) hot tea
- 1 orange slice

Pour the liqueur into a tall glass (with a silver spoon in it to prevent the glass from cracking). Add hot tea. Stir. Slip in the orange slice as garnish.

Jack Rose

- 3 ounces (90ml) calvados (or apple brandy)
- Juice of 1 lemon
- 1 teaspoon grenadine

Shake with ice, and pour into a cocktail glass.

Kiss-me-quick highball

- 2 dashes aromatic bitters
- 1¹/₂ ounces (45ml) of Pernod
- 4 dashes curaçao
- Soda water

Place the first three ingredients in a highball glass with cracked ice. Top with soda water and serve.

Margarita

- 2 ounces (60ml) tequila
- ¹/₂ ounce (15ml) Cointreau or Triple Sec
- 1 tablespoon lime juice

Combine in mixing glass, stir with ice then drain. Classically the glass should have its rim rubbed with lime and dipped into salt. I prefer my Margaritas unadorned and unsalted.

Mocha Flip

- 2 ounces (60ml) Kahlua or Tia Maria
- Yolk of 1 egg
- 1 tablespoon heavy cream
- ¹/₂ cup shaved ice
- Grated nutmeg

Place the first four ingredients in a blender for 20 seconds (or shake very well). Serve in a wine glass with a sprinkle of nutmeg as a seductive after-dinner drink.

Newton's Apple

- *1¹/₂ ounces (45ml) calvados or apple brandy*
- *¹/₂ ounce (15ml) curaçao*
- *2 dashes Angostura bitters*

Shake hard with crushed ice, and strain into cocktail glasses.

Nightcap

- *1 glass cold milk*
- *1 whole egg*
- *2 tablespoons honey or brown sugar*
- *2 ounces (60ml) cognac*

Beat or blend the milk, egg and honey. Add the cognac. Stir and serve at bedtime in a tall glass, and Z-z-z!

Paris Opera Special

- *1¹/₂ ounces (45ml) grapefruit juice*
- *1¹/₂ ounces (45ml) blue curaçao*
- *1 ounce (30ml) white rum*

Stir the ingredients with ice in a tall glass.

Pear With Lime

- *2 ounces (60ml) Swiss Poire Williams*
- *¹/₂ ounce (15ml) (or to taste) lime juice (with sugar if you use fresh limes)*
- *A squirt of soda water*
- *Ice*

Mix in a glass. A sultry Swiss once introduced Poire Williams to me this way, for which I have been ever grateful!

Pernorange

- 2 ounces (60ml) orange juice
- 1 ounce (30ml) Pernod

Serve in a tall glass with ice.

Piña Borracha

- 3 cups fresh pineapple chunks
- 1 bottle tequila

Pour into a large jar with sealable lid. Cover securely; leave in refrigerator for 24 hours. Strain and rebottle. Serve as a liqueur. This is less well known than Piña Colada, and easier to make.

Pink Panther

- 2 ounces (60ml) Pernod
- 1 dash grenadine
- Soda water

Shake the Pernod and grenadine with ice and top up with soda water in an Old Fashioned glass. (As served at St George's Bar, Brown's Hotel.)

Quickie

- 1½ ounces (45ml) port wine
- 1½ ounces (45ml) Grand Marnier
- 2 dashes Angostura bitters

Shake well with crushed ice, strain into a cocktail glass.

The Rocket

- 1 ounce (30ml) acquavit
- 1 ounce (30ml) kummël

Pour from ice-cold bottles into cocktail glasses. Stir.

Ridley

- 1 ounce (30ml) tequila
- 1 ounce (30ml) gin
- 1 dash Galliano

Pour the tequila and gin into a tall glass filled with crushed ice. Top with Galliano. (Blake's Hotel, with its profusion of plants, modern decor and swift, silent service, is the perfect setting for this their speciality.)

Royal Silver

- 1 ounce (30ml) Poire Williams
- 1 ounce (30ml) Cointreau
- 2 ounces (60ml) grapefruit juice
- Champagne

Shake the first three ingredients with ice, strain into a cocktail glass with sugar round the rim, then top up with champagne. (Vic at the Savoy Bar will make this for you at the drop of a hint!)

Sidecar

- 2 ounces (60ml) brandy
- 1 ounce (30ml) Cointreau or Triple Sec
- Juice of ¹/₂ a lemon

Shake with ice, then strain into a sugar-rimmed cocktail glass.

Steadier

- *2 ounces (60ml) brandy*
- *2 dashes curaçao*
- *2 dashes Angostura bitters*
- *Lemon twist*

Stir with ice, serve with a twist of lemon. A good steadier for shaky nerves.

Time Bomb

- *1 ounce (30ml) aquavit*
- *1 ounce (30ml) vodka*
- *1 ounce (30ml) lemon juice*
- *1 twist lemon zest*

Mix in a large cocktail glass. For a real connoisseur of dry drinks.

Stinger

- *1¹/₂ ounces (45ml) brandy*
- *1¹/₂ ounces (45ml) crème de menthe (white)*

Shake with crushed ice. Usually an after-dinner drink. As a cocktail, before dinner, use 2 ounces (60ml) brandy to 1 ounce (30ml) crème de menthe, to reduce sweetness. Serve in an Old Fashioned glass.

Tiger Tail

- *2 ounces (60ml) Pernod*
- *8 ounces (250ml) cold orange juice*

Mix in a tall glass and stir.

Valencia

- *2 ounces (60ml) apricot brandy*
- *1 ounce (30ml) orange juice*
- *4 dashes orange bitters*
- *Champagne or sparkling wine (optional)*

Stir the first three ingredients well with ice. Serve in a tall glass and fill with champagne or sparkling wine.

PUNCHES

Punch was a staple accompaniment to most social **gatherings in** the days of Nicholas Nickleby and Mr. Pickwick. Today punch still adds to the general hospitality of special occasions with strong implications of friendliness and welcome. Punch was a forebear of cocktails, some of which are simply small individual punches, a Bellini (peach juice and champagne) for instance. There are spirituous, strong punches, and mild wine-based, even tee-total, ones. People sometimes become anxious about the unknown potency of a punch, so at a party you should provide plain whisky and soda or soft drinks on the side, to cater for the timid.

Champagne punch is the highpoint of this mixed beverage art – traditional for weddings, dances, birthday parties, anniversaries, and suchlike. Since it requires a mixture of ingredients, you need not use expensive champagne. Use sparkling wine in its place, as long as the bubbly part remains prominent. Champagne for a punch should be dry, or medium dry, thoroughly chilled, and only added to the rest of the ingredients at the last minute.

Punches can be cold for summer parties, or hot in winter. Summer ones are inclined to be wine, gin or vodka based. Winter calls for rum, whisky or brandy. Hot punches used to be the correct thing to serve to carol singers at Christmas time to warm them up – heady mixtures like Brandy Bishops, Hot Buttered Rum or Hot Toddies, filled with spices.

For cold punch, a large block of ice in a punch bowl makes a more efficacious coolant than ice cubes. It melts less fast, so does not dilute the drink, and makes it easier to use a ladle for serving. Actually, you can freeze the ingredients (tea, for example, or fruit juices) that contain no alcohol, and use them instead of the ice block. Hot punches should be served from metal bowls to avoid the possibility of cracking china or glass.

One gallon (4.55 litres) of punch will make about 32 glasses or cups – for ten to twelve people. Get your ingredients ready and test your mixtures well in advance of needing them.

Bloodshot

- 1 measure vodka
- 1 measure tomato juice
- 1 measure canned consommé
- Juice of ¹/₂ lemon
- Dash of Worcestershire sauce

Stir and serve in Old Fashioned glasses with ice.

Bowle

- 2 pounds (1 kg) fresh strawberries
- Sugar
- 1 bottle white wine
- 3 bottles champagne or sparkling wine

Slice half the strawberries and add sugar to taste in a mixing bowl. Pour in the white wine (moselle or hock are good). Macerate for 2 hours or even overnight. Strain and pour into a punch bowl over a block of ice. Just before serving slice and add the remaining strawberries and the sparkling white wine or champagne.

Serves about 24 in wine glasses. Bowles can be made with other soft fruit such as peaches, in the same way. A small handful of fresh woodruff in the maceration adds a spring-like taste.

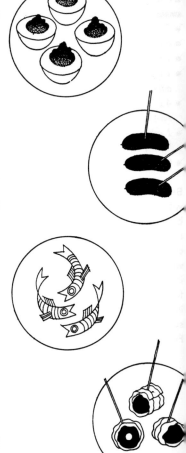

Brandy Eggnog

- 2 eggs, separated
- 6 teaspoons sugar
- 1 bottle brandy
- 1 quart (1.2 litres) milk
- 4 ounces (120ml) dark rum
- 1 quart (1.2 litres) lightly whipped cream
- Grated nutmeg

Beat the yolks lightly with sugar. While beating add the brandy, milk, rum and whipped cream. Whisk the egg whites until stiff and fold into the mixture. Chill for several hours. Serve in wine glasses and sprinkle with nutmeg. For 25.

Champagne Cooler

- 1/2 bottle Sauternes
- Juice of 1 lemon
- 1/2 pint (300ml) pineapple juice
- 2 ounces (60g) castor sugar
- 1 bottle dry champagne
- Sticks of fresh pineapple

Mix thoroughly the Sauternes, lemon and pineapple juice, and the sugar. Divide equally into eight or ten highball glasses, filled with ice. Top glasses up with champagne (the ice will melt somewhat). Garnish with sticks of pineapple.

Champagne Cup

- 4 ounces (120ml) brandy
- 2 ounces (60ml) curaçao
- 2 ounces (60ml) maraschino
- 1 quart (1.2 litres) cider
- 6 dashes grenadine
- Orange slices
- Lemon slices
- Pineapple
- Cucumber slices
- 3 – 4 mint sprigs
- 1 bottle champagne

Mix or shake the first five ingredients well in a large glass jug full of ice. Decorate with the orange, lemon, pineapple, cucumber and sprigs of mint. Finally, and without stirring any further, pour in the champagne. If the party likes things sweet, you can also add a teaspoon or so of sugar.

Christmas Punch

Basic version
- 1 bottle Rye whiskey
- 2 ounces (60ml) Southern Comfort
- 2 ounces (60ml) dark rum
- 2 medium sized lumps rock candy
- 2 quarters each of lemon and orange, stuck with cloves
- Cinnamon

Additional for hot version per glass
- Juice of one lemon
- 1 teaspoon honey
- 1 lemon slice with clove in it
- 1 stick of cinnamon

Blend whiskey, Southern Comfort and rum and pour into screw-top jars. Add rock candy and fruit and cinnamon. Leave for 4 weeks. (If fruit has discoloured, strain off the liquid and add fresh fruit, fresh cloves and cinnamon before serving.) To serve cold, simply pour, strained, into liqueur glasses and sip. To serve hot, put two ounces (60ml) – more or less, according to your taste – of the marinated liquid into each of several glasses. Add to each lemon juice, honey and a cinnamon stick. Place a silver spoon in each glass and fill with hot water. You can decorate this with slices of fruit if you like. Vic, at the Savoy Bar, points out that you'd better set about making this on November 25th!

Cool Summer Salad

- *1 pound (500g) strawberries*
- *Juice of 2 oranges*
- *1 bottle dry cider*

Wash and slice the strawberries. Soak in the orange juice for 1 hour. Pour in cider and stir. Add ice and serve in tall glasses. (If there are any strawberries left over, eat them with cream – they're delicious!)

Fruit Juice Cup

- *3 cups lemon juice*
- *1 quart (1.2 litres) orange juice*
- *1 cup pineapple juice*
- *1 cup simple syrup*
- *2 quarts (2.4 litres) ginger ale*
- *Orange slices*
- *Lemon slices*

Mix the fruit juices and sugar syrup together. Pour over ice in a punch bowl. Add the ginger ale and garnish with fruit slices. (This can easily be turned into something much stronger by adding 2 ounces (60ml) of vodka, gin, rum or whisky to each serving. Vodka mixes best with almost any kind of fruit juice taste.) Serve in a wine glass or punch cup.

Glögg

- 1 bottle dry red wine
- 1 bottle Sauternes
- 1 bottle sweet vermouth
- 15 cloves
- 1 stick cinnamon
- 1/2 cup aquavit
- 1/2 pound (250g) sugar lumps
- 1 cup raisins
- 1 cup almonds (blanched)

Heat all ingredients but aquavit, raisins, almonds and sugar in a large pot (do not boil). When hot, line up sugar lumps on a rack over the pot. Pour warmed aquavit over sugar, stand back, and set alight. Ladle the mixture over sugar until flames go out. Serve in mugs with a few raisins and almonds in each. (Serves 8 – 12.)

Glühwein (or Mull)

- 4 ounces (120ml) dry red wine
- 2 – 3 cloves
- Small piece of cinnamon stick
- Twist of lemon peel
- 1 teaspoon castor sugar
- 1 dash Angostura bitters
- 1 pinch allspice

Heat all the ingredients in a pot (without boiling). Strain into a mug or a glass with silver spoon in it.

Hintelsham's Coffee Punch

- *1 bottle Marc de Bourgogne (or any brandy)*
- *1/2 pint (300ml) strong black coffee*
- *Juice of 1 lemon*
- *1/4 pound (120g) sugar*
- *Instant coffee grains*

Slightly warm the brandy then set alight in a metal bowl. Pour in the coffee and stir, then add the lemon and sugar. While the concoction is still burning, sprinkle with instant coffee granules for added sparkle. (Has nice pyrotechnic effects – a festive way to end a feast.) Serves 6 in punch cups or wine glasses.

Hot Buttered Rum

- *2 ounces (60ml) dark rum*
- *1 stick cinnamon*
- *Twist lemon peel*
- *2 cloves*
- *1 bottle cider (or water)*
- *1 tablespoon unsalted butter*
- *Sugar*
- *Nutmeg*

Place rum, cinnamon, lemon peel and cloves in large mug (or metal tankard). Heat the cider (or water) to boiling. Pour over the ingredients in the mug and add the butter. Stir, adding sugar to taste. Grate nutmeg over the top.

Lemonade Punch

- 2 quarts (2.4 litres) strong tea
- Juice of 6 lemons
- 1 cup sugar
- Springs of mint
- 1 quart (1.2 litres) ginger ale

Cool the tea and add lemon juice, sugar and mint. Just before serving add the ginger ale. (A good beverage for those who do not 'drink', but you can add 2 ounces (60ml) of rum or vodka if you want to make it alcoholic. Serve in tall glasses.

Love Potion

- 1 pound (500g) sugar
- 1 teaspoon powdered nutmeg
- 2 teaspoons ground ginger
- 6 whole cloves
- 1/2 teaspoon mace
- 6 whole allspice
- 1 teaspoon ground cinnamon
- 1/2 pint (300ml) water
- 4 bottles medium dry sherry
- 12 eggs, separated

Mix dry ingredients in the water in a large saucepan. Add the sherry and heat gently. Beat the egg yolks and whisk the whites until stiff. Add both to the brew and serve.

Planter's Punch

- Juice of 1 lime
- 2 teaspoons castor sugar, or simple syrup
- 2 ounces (60ml) rum (usually dark)
- 1 dash Angostura bitters
- Soda water
- Orange slice
- Maraschino cherry

Fill a tall glass 3/4 full of crushed ice. Pour in the first four ingredients. Stir until the glass is frosted. Top up with soda water, and stir to mix. Serve with a slice of orange and maraschino cherry, if desired.

Port in a Storm

- 4 ounces (120ml) port
- 1 – 2 dashes brandy
- Juice of ¹/₂ lemon

Use an ordinary ruby port since it is a mixed drink. Stir well with ice and drink on the rocks or strained in a wine glass.

Rhine Wine Punch

- 2 quarts (2.4 litres) of Rhine wine or moselle
- 2 quarts (2.4 litres) soda water
- 4 ounces (120ml) brandy
- 4 ounces (120ml) curaçao
- 4 ounces (120ml) Benedictine
- Juice of 4 lemons
- Apples, sliced
- Oranges, sliced
- Pineapple, chopped
- Mint sprigs

Pour the first six ingredients over an ice block. Float slices of fruit and sprigs of mint on top in wine glasses. (Serves 12 – 16).

Sangria

- 1 quart (1.2litres) red wine (Spanish preferably)
- 1 orange, sliced
- 1 lime, sliced
- 1 lemon, sliced
- Juice of 1 lemon
- Juice of 1 orange
- 1 teaspoon simple syrup, or castor sugar (to taste)
- 1 quart (1.2litres) soda water

Pour all the ingredients into a large pitcher. Stir and add a trayful of ice cubes. Serve in red wine glasses. (For 8 – 10 people.)

(If you want a more powerful punch, add 1 ounce (30ml) of brandy per glass – again Spanish, preferably. The simple wine version is best for luncheon-time or summer drinking.) This punch is a visual as well as a sensual treat.

Sangaree is a colonial American version of Sangria, made with fresh lemonade, a little sugar, ice, 'spring water', and port, sherry or red wine. Add lemonade and wine in equal parts. Add slices of lemon or orange, and a dash of nutmeg. Serve in tall glasses.

Sherry Flip

- *2 ounces (60ml) medium sherry*
- *1 teaspoon castor sugar*
- *1 egg*
- *4 dashes crème de cacao*
- *Nutmeg*

Place all the ingredients with ½ cup cracked ice in a blender. Blend to a sherbet-like consistency. Pour into frosted cocktail glasses and top with a pinch of nutmeg.

Summer Punch

- *1 gallon (4.55 litres) dry white wine*
- *1 bottle vodka*
- *1 cup green tea*
- *3 lemons, sliced*

Mix and (if you want the strength increased) add a cup of rum or brandy. (Serves 12 – 14). Pour over a block of ice. This punch for outdoor living can be made in advance.

Trinidad Rum Punch

- 1 quart (1.2 litres) water
- 1½ pounds (750g) sugar
- 1 bottle dark Caribbean rum
- Juice of 8 limes or lemons
- Several dashes of Angostura bitters
- Nutmeg or ginger

Heat the water until boiling and add the sugar. Stir until dissolved, then add the rum, lime juice and Angostura. Serve cold in tall glasses, or hot (in metal containers please) with a red hot poker thrust into the middle, thus producing an impressive audio-visual effect. Sprinkle each drink with nutmeg or ginger. (A perfect example of punch that improves with age. It can be drunk right away. Kept in the fridge for a while, it tastes even better!)

Tea Punch

- 2 cans frozen lemon juice
- 1 can frozen orange juice
- 1½ quarts (1.8 litres) strong tea, cooled
- 1 bottle vodka
- Lemon slices
- Orange slices
- Strawberries

Mix the first four ingredients. Just before serving pour over an ice block and add the fruit. Its impact is nice and sour-dry, but you can add sugar if you like. Good for about ten tennis buffs! Serve in tall glasses.

Wassail

Version 1

- 6 pints (3.6 litres) beer or ale
- $^1/_4$ pound (120g) sugar
- 8 ounces (250ml) sherry
- Grated nutmeg
- Ginger

Mix 1 pint (600ml) of beer with the sugar, sherry and spices. Stir in the remaining beer and leave to stand for 2 to 3 hours.

Like rum punch there are dozens of recipes for this concoction. Wassail was originally a toast – 'was hael' meaning 'your good health' in Old English – and perhaps the most authentic version was this one drunk at Oxford centuries ago. Serve in punch cups or wine glasses.

Version 2

A more recent version, unknown to ancient drinkers, eliminates the beer altogether and uses instead:

- 1 pound (500g) sugar
- 1 teaspoon powdered nutmeg
- 2 teaspoons powdered ginger
- 6 whole allspice
- 1 teaspoon cinnamon
- $^1/_2$ pint (300ml) water
- 4 bottles sherry
- 12 eggs, separated
- 12 apples

Mix the dry ingredients with the water in a saucepan. Add the sherry and heat gently. Beat the egg yolks and whisk the whites until stiff. Add to the heated brew. Finally, bake the apples in a moderate oven for 20 minutes. Float them on top and serve in punch cups.

Acapulco 54
ale 77
Alexander 24
Algonquin 54
Amaretto almond liqueur 33
Angostura bitters 11, 18, 28, 35, 36, 37, 40, 43, 44, 50, 51, 55, 60, 61, 63, 70, 72, 76,
anisette 41, 51
aperitifs 53
apple brandy 13, 53, 54, 58, 60
apple juice 37
apricot brandy 11, 26, 40, 48, 50, 63
Aqua Marina 32
aquavit 53, 62, 63, 70
armagnac brandy 53
arrack 53

B & B 55
Bacardi Cocktail 48
barspoon measure 12
beef bouillon 32
beer 40, 77
Bellini 16, 21, 65
Benedictine 11, 55, 73
bitters 11, 13, 19, 23, 41, 42, 59, 63
  see also Angostura bitters
Black Velvet 16
Bloodshot 66
Bloody Mary 33
Blue Champagne 16
blue curaçao 16, 29, 55, 60
Blue Med 55
Boilermaker 40
Bossa Nova 48
bourbon whiskey 11, 42, 43, 44
Bowle 66

brandy 11, 13, 18, 24, 52-63, 60, 62, 63, 65, 67, 71, 73, 75
Brandy Bishop 65
Brandy Eggnog 67
Brandy Sling 55
Brandy Smash 55
Braniff Special 56
Bronx 24
Buck's Fizz 17
Bulldog Cooler 24
Bullshot 32
burgundy 15

Café Kirsch 56
calvados 37, 53, 58, 60
  see also apple brandy
Calypso 48
Campari 25, 28, 53
Cardinal 25
Chambery dry vermouth 25
champagne 11, 14 – 21, 32, 62, 63, 65, 66, 67
  Bollinger 17
Champagne Cobbler 17
Champagne Cocktail 18
Champagne Cooler 67
Champagne Cup 67
Champagne Pick-Me-Up 19
Champagne Punch 65
Champerno 19
charteuse 11
  green, yellow 26
Chicago 19
Chocolate Cocktail 49
Christmas Punch 68
cider 67, 69, 71
cocktails 13, 15, 18, 48, 51, 53, 57, 65
coconut cream 50, 54

coffee 56, 71
coffee liqueur 54
Coffee Royale 56
cognac brandy 11, 13, 19, 53, 55, 56, 60
cointreau 11, 29, 34, 40, 57, 58, 59, 62
cola 13, 49
collins 13, 29, 35, 51
collins measure 12
consommé, canned 66
Cooch Behar 32
Cool Summer Salad 69
coolers 13, 24, 36, 37, 67
cream 15, 24, 49, 58, 59, 67
crème de cacao 11, 24, 75
crème de cassis 11, 20
crème de menthe 11, 32, 34, 49, 57, 63
Crème de Menthe Frappé 57
Crimean Cocktail 57
Cuba Libre 49
cucumber 35, 67
curaçao 11, 16, 17, 19, 28, 49, 59, 60, 63, 67, 73
  blue curaçao 16, 29, 55, 60

Daiquiri 49
dash, measure 12
Drambuie 11, 35, 57
Dry Martini 5, 12, 23, 25
Dubonnet 34, 51
Duke, The 57

Eau-de-vie 11
eau-de-vie fraises 21
eggs 13, 26, 29, 36, 44, 49, 51, 56, 57, 59, 60, 67, 72, 75, 77
equipment 6

Euphoria 49
Fernet Branca 19, 53
flips 13, 59, 75
Flying Red Horse 33
Flying Scot 40
Football Fan 40
Fourth of July 40
framboise 21
frappés 13, 53, 57
French '75 20
Fruit Juice Cup 69
fruit juices 6, 13, 53, 72
  see also lemon juice, lime
  juice etc.

Galliano 11, 34, 48, 58, 62
gazpacho 37
Gibson 25
gin 11, 12, 13, 22 – 29, 36, 37,
  62, 65, 69
  Plymouth gin 28
Gin Buck 25
ginger ale 11, 13, 24, 25, 69, 72
glassware 8, 9, 10
Glögg 70
Gloom Raiser 26
Glühwein 70
Godmother, The 33
Golden Dawn 26
Golden Dream 58
Golden Fizz 26
Grand Marnier 11, 33, 43, 56, 61
grape juice 21
grapefruit juice 40, 49, 60, 62
Greek Manhattan 58
Green Lady 26
Green Treetop 34
grenadine 11, 16, 26, 27, 33, 35,
  37, 44, 45, 48, 51, 58, 61, 67

grogs 5
Guinness 16

Hair Raiser 34
Harry Lauder 40
Harvey Wallbanger 34
highball measure 12
highballs 13, 59
Hintelsham's Coffee Punch 71
honey 60, 68
Hot Buttered Rum 65, 71
Hot-T 58
Hot Toddy 65
Hurricane, The 50

Irish whiskey 45

Jack Rose 58
jigger measure 12
juleps 13, 42

Kahlua 54, 59
Kir Royale 20
kirsch 21, 53, 56
Kiss-Me-Quick Highball 59
Kojak 41
kümmel 11, 62

Ladies' 41
Leave It To Me 27
Le Mans 34
lemon juice 13, 17, 24, 27, 29,
  32, 34, 35, 36, 40, 44, 45, 49,
  50, 51, 55, 56, 62, 63, 66, 67,
  68, 69, 71, 72, 73, 74, 76
Lemonade Punch 72
Lillet dry vermouth 25, 53
lime juice 13, 26, 29, 36, 44, 45,
  47, 48, 49, 51, 59, 60, 72, 76

Loch Lomond 41
Love Potion 72
Lovers' Nocturne 35
Lucky Jim 35

Maiden's Blush 27
Manhattan 41, 42
maraschino 11, 27, 43, 53, 67
Margarita 59
measurements 12
Metaxas brandy 58
milk 60, 67
Mimosa 15
mint 13, 34, 35, 37, 42, 50, 55,
  56, 67, 72, 73
Mint Collins 35
Mint Julep 42
Mocha Flip 59
Mojito 50
Monkey Gland 27
Morton's Special 35
Mull 70

Negroni 28
New Yorker 44
Newton's Apple 60
Nightcap 60
Noilly Prat dry vermouth 25

Old Fashioned 43
orange juice 15, 17, 24, 26, 27,
  28, 33, 34, 35, 40, 48, 55, 57,
  58, 61, 63, 69, 74, 76
Oriental Cooler 36
ouzo 55

Paradise 50
Paris Opera Special 60
passionfruit juice 41, 50

peach juice 16, 65
Pear with Lime 60
Pernod 11, 26, 27, 41, 53, 55, 59, 61, 63
Pernorange 61
Piña Borracha 61
Piña Colada 50, 61
pinch, measure 12
Pineapple Collins 51
pineapple juice 41, 48, 49, 50, 51, 67, 69
Pink Elephant 44
Pink Gin 28
Pink Panther 61
pinks, Ratafia of 36
Planter's Punch 51, 72
Poire Williams 53, 60, 62
pony measure 12
Port in a Storm 73
port wine 13, 61, 73, 74
punches 13, 51, 64 – 77

Quickie 61

Raspberries 36
Raspberry Vodka 36
Ratafia of Pinks 36
retsina 5
Rhine Wine Punch 73
Ridley 62
Rob Roy 44
Rocket, The 62
Ron Cacique 51
Royal Silver 62
rum 11, 13, 29, 46 – 51, 65, 69, 71, 76
    Bacardi 47
    dark rum 41, 47, 49, 50, 51, 54, 67, 68, 71, 72, 76

Jamaica rum 47
    light rum 47, 48, 51
    white rum 49, 50, 60
rye whiskey 39, 42, 43, 68

Sangaree 74
Sangria 74
Sauternes 67, 70
Scotch Mist 45
Shanghai Cocktail 51
sherry 13, 37, 53, 72, 74, 75, 77
Sherry Flip 75
Sidecar 62
Silver Vodka Fizz 36
simple syrup 11, 24, 40, 48, 49, 51, 69, 72, 74
slings 13, 55
sours 13, 45
Southern Comfort 53, 68
Steadier 63
Stinger 63
'stir or shake' 13
strawberries 15, 21, 56, 66, 69, 76
Strawberry Champagne Delight 21
Summer of '75 37
Summer Punch 75
Swedish punch 11

Tabasco 32
Tango 28
tea 58, 65, 72, 76
Tea Punch 76
teaspoon measure 12
Tequila 11, 35, 50, 53, 54, 59, 61, 62
Tia Maria 54, 59
Tiger Tail 63

Time Bomb 63
Titiani 16, 21
toddies 13, 65
Tom Collins 29
tomato juice 11, 32, 66
tonic water 11, 34, 36
Trinidad Rum Punch 76
Triple Sec 11, 59, 62

Valencia 63
vermouth 11, 12, 13, 23, 53
    dry 24, 25, 26, 28, 35, 41, 44
    French dry 23
    Italian red 23, 42
    Italian white 23
    sweet 28, 40, 70
vodka 11, 23, 29, 30 – 37, 55, 63, 65, 66, 69, 72, 75, 76
    coloured vodka 31, 33
Vodkatina Dry 37
Vodpacho 37

Wallis Blue 29
Wassail 77
Watermelon Cooler 37
whisky 11, 13, 29, 38 – 45, 65, 69
Whisky Sour 45
White Lady 29
White Irish Rose 45
Wild Irish Rose 45
Williams fruit brandy 21, 53
wine 13, 65
    red 15, 58, 70, 74
    sparkling 15, 63, 65, 66
    white 57, 66, 67, 73, 75
wine glass measure 12
Worcestershire sauce 32, 66

Zubrovka 31